U.S. Department of Justice
Office of Justice Programs
National Institute of Justice

I0476930

National Institute of Justice

Law Enforcement and Corrections Standards and Testing Program

Color Test Reagents/Kits for Preliminary Identification of Drugs of Abuse

NIJ Standard–0604.01

ABOUT THE LAW ENFORCEMENT AND CORRECTIONS STANDARDS AND TESTING PROGRAM

The Law Enforcement and Corrections Standards and Testing Program is sponsored by the Office of Science and Technology of the National Institute of Justice (NIJ), U.S. Department of Justice. The program responds to the mandate of the Justice System Improvement Act of 1979, which directed NIJ to encourage research and development to improve the criminal justice system and to disseminate the results to Federal, State, and local agencies.

The Law Enforcement and Corrections Standards and Testing Program is an applied research effort that determines the technological needs of justice system agencies, sets minimum performance standards for specific devices, tests commercially available equipment against those standards, and disseminates the standards and the test results to criminal justice agencies nationally and internationally.

The program operates through:

The *Law Enforcement and Corrections Technology Advisory Council* (LECTAC), consisting of nationally recognized criminal justice practitioners from Federal, State, and local agencies, which assesses technological needs and sets priorities for research programs and items to be evaluated and tested.

The *Office of Law Enforcement Standards* (OLES) at the National Institute of Standards and Technology, which develops voluntary national performance standards for compliance testing to ensure that individual items of equipment are suitable for use by criminal justice agencies. The standards are based upon laboratory testing and evaluation of representative samples of each item of equipment to determine the key attributes, develop test methods, and establish minimum performance requirements for each essential attribute. In addition to the highly technical standards, OLES also produces technical reports and user guidelines that explain in nontechnical terms the capabilities of available equipment.

The *National Law Enforcement and Corrections Technology Center (NLECTC),* operated by a grantee, which supervises a national compliance testing program conducted by independent laboratories. The standards developed by OLES serve as performance benchmarks against which commercial equipment is measured. The facilities, personnel, and testing capabilities of the independent laboratories are evaluated by OLES prior to testing each item of equipment, and OLES helps the NLECTC staff review and analyze data. Test results are published in Equipment Performance Reports designed to help justice system procurement officials make informed purchasing decisions.

Publications are available at no charge through the National Law Enforcement and Corrections Technology Center. Some documents are also available online through the Internet/World Wide Web. To request a document or additional information, call 800–248–2742 or 301–519–5060, or write:

National Law Enforcement and Corrections Technology Center
P.O. Box 1160
Rockville, MD 20849–1160
E-Mail: *asknlectc@nlectc.org*
World Wide Web address: *http://www.nlectc.org*

The National Institute of Justice is a component of the Office of Justice Programs, which also includes the Bureau of Justice Assistance, the Bureau of Justice Statistics, the Office of Juvenile Justice and Delinquency Prevention, and the Office for Victims of Crime.

U.S. Department of Justice
Office of Justice Programs
National Institute of Justice

Color Test Reagents/Kits for Preliminary Identification of Drugs of Abuse

NIJ Standard–0604.01

Supersedes NILECJ–STD–0604.01, Chemical Spot Test Kits for Preliminary Identification of Drugs of Abuse, dated December 1978, and NIJ Standard–0605.00, Color Test Reagents/Kits for Preliminary Identification of Drugs of Abuse, dated July 1981

Coordination by:
National Institute of Standards and Technology
Office of Law Enforcement Standards
Gaithersburg, MD 20899–8102

Prepared for:
National Institute of Justice
Office of Science and Technology
Washington, DC 20531

July 2000

NCJ 183258

National Institute of Justice

Julie E. Samuels
Acting Director

The technical effort to develop this report was conducted
under Interagency Agreement 94–IJ–R–004,
Project No. 97–028–CTT.

This standard was formulated by the Office of Law Enforcement
Standards (OLES) of the National Institute of Standards
and Technology (NIST) under the direction of
Alim A. Fatah, Program Manager for Chemical Systems
and Materials, and Kathleen M. Higgins, Director of OLES.
Revision of this standard was performed at the
University of Utah, Center for Human Toxicology (CHT)
by Dennis J. Crouch, Interim Director of CHT.

The work resulting from this report was sponsored by the
National Institute of Justice (NIJ), David G. Boyd, Director,
Office of Science and Technology.

FOREWORD

This document, NIJ Standard" 0604.01, Color Test Reagents/Kits for Preliminary Identification of Drugs of Abuse, is an equipment standard developed by the Office of Law Enforcement Standards of the National Institute of Standards and Technology. It was produced as part of the Law Enforcement and Corrections Standards and Testing Program of the National Institute of Justice. A brief description of the program appears on the inside front cover.

This standard is a technical document that specifies performance and other requirements equipment should meet to satisfy the needs of criminal justice agencies for high-quality service. Purchasers can use the test methods described in this standard to determine whether a particular piece of equipment meets the essential requirements, or they may have the tests conducted on their behalf by a qualified testing laboratory. Procurement officials may also refer to this standard in their purchasing documents and require that equipment offered for purchase meet the requirements. Compliance with the requirements of the standard may be attested to by an independent laboratory or guaranteed by the vendor.

Because this NIJ standard is designed as a procurement aid, it is necessarily highly technical. For those who seek general guidance concerning the selection and application of law enforcement equipment, user guides have also been published. The guides explain in nontechnical language how to select equipment capable of the performance required by an agency.

NIJ standards are subjected to continuing review. Technical comments and recommended revisions are welcome. Please send suggestions to the Director, Office of Science and Technology, National Institute of Justice, U.S. Department of Justice, Washington, DC 20531.

Before citing this or any other NIJ standard in a contract document, users should verify that the most recent edition of the standard is used. Write to: Director, Office of Law Enforcement Standards, National Institute of Standards and Technology, Gaithersburg, MD 20899–8102.

David G. Boyd, Director
Office of Science and Technology
National Institute of Justice

CONTENTS

FOREWORD.. iii

COMMONLY USED SYMBOLS AND ABBREVIATIONS... vi

1. PURPOSE 1

2. SCOPE 1

3. DEFINITIONS.. 1

   3.1 Munsell Color Charts 1

   3.2 Centroid Color Charts 2

   3.3 Final Color.. 2

4. REQUIREMENTS... 2

   4.1 User Information 2

   4.2 Labeling 7

   4.3 Workmanship 7

   4.4 Safe-Disposal Materials 7

   4.5 Color Samples 7

   4.6 Test Color and Sensitivity 8

   4.7 Drug Detection Limit 8

   4.8 Specificity 8

5. TEST METHODS.. 8

   5.1 General Test Conditions 8

   5.2 Test Color 8

   5.3 Drug Detection Limit Determination 9

   5.4 Specificity Test 9

APPENDIX A–REAGENTS 12

APPENDIX B–SAFETY PRECAUTIONS... 14

APPENDIX C–STORAGE PRECAUTIONS.. 18

TABLES

Table 1. Final colors produced by reagents A.l through A.2 with various drugs and
         other substances... 3

Table 2. Drug detection limits 10

Table 3. Specificity of color tests 11

COMMONLY USED SYMBOLS AND ABBREVIATIONS

A	ampere	H	henry	nm	nanometer
ac	alternating current	h	hour	No.	number
AM	amplitude modulation	hf	high frequency	o.d.	outside diameter
cd	candela	Hz	hertz	Ω	ohm
cm	centimeter	i.d.	inside diameter	p.	page
CP	chemically pure	in	inch	Pa	pascal
c/s	cycle per second	IR	infrared	pe	probable error
d	day	J	joule	pp.	pages
dB	decibel	L	lambert	ppm	parts per million
dc	direct current	L	liter	qt	quart
°C	degree Celsius	lb	pound	rad	radian
°F	degree Fahrenheit	lbf	pound-force	rf	radio frequency
dia	diameter	lbf·in	pound-force inch	rh	relative humidity
emf	electromotive force	lm	lumen	s	second
eq	equation	ln	logarithm (base e)	SD	standard deviation
F	farad	log	logarithm (base 10)	sec.	section
fc	footcandle	M	molar	SWR	standing wave ratio
fig.	figure	m	meter	uhf	ultrahigh frequency
FM	frequency modulation	min	minute	UV	ultraviolet
ft	foot	mm	millimeter	V	volt
ft/s	foot per second	mph	miles per hour	vhf	very high frequency
g	acceleration	m/s	meter per second	W	watt
g	gram	N	newton	λ	wavelength
gr	grain	N·m	newton meter	wt	weight

area=unit^2 (e.g., ft^2, in^2, etc.); volume=unit^3 (e.g., ft^3, m^3, etc.)

PREFIXES

d	deci (10^{-1})	da	deka (10)
c	centi (10^{-2})	h	hecto (10^2)
m	milli (10^{-3})	k	kilo (10^3)
μ	micro (10^{-6})	M	mega (10^6)
n	nano (10^{-9})	G	giga (10^9)
p	pico (10^{-12})	T	tera (10^{1012})

COMMON CONVERSIONS
(See ASTM E380)

0.30480 m =1ft	4.448222 N = lbf
2.54 cm = 1 in	1.355818 J =1 ft·lbf
0.4535924 kg = 1 lb	0.1129848 N m = lbf·in
0.06479891g = 1gr	14.59390 N/m =1 lbf/ft
0.9463529 L = 1 qt	6894.757 Pa = 1 lbf/in^2
3600000 J = 1 kW·hr	1.609344 km/h = mph

Temperature: $T_C = (T_F - 32) \times 5/9$
Temperature: $T_F = (T_C \times 9/5) + 32$

vi

NIJ STANDARD
FOR
COLOR TEST REAGENTS/KITS FOR
PRELIMINARY IDENTIFICATION
OF DRUGS OF ABUSE

1. PURPOSE

The purpose of this standard is to establish minimum requirements for color test reagent/kits to detect drugs of abuse and methods of testing the reagents to determine compliance with those requirements.

2. SCOPE

This standard applies to field-testing kits that consist of color test reagents for the preliminary identification of drugs of abuse (hereinafter referred to simply as drugs) in their pure and/or diluted forms. It does not apply to kits that use thin layer chromatography as the identification procedure nor to kits that identify drugs in body fluids.

This standard supersedes NILECJ–STD–0604.00, "Chemical Spot Test Kits for Preliminary Identification of Drugs of Abuse," December 1978, and NIJ Standard–0605.00, "Color Test Reagents/Kits for Preliminary Identification of Drugs of Abuse," July 1981. The standard is concerned with single reagents (or reagent combinations) used to give a preliminary identi-fication of a suspected drug or class of drugs in their pure and/or diluted forms.

Note that this standard does not mandate the identities of the reagents to be included in a test kit. Since they are among the reagents currently in most common use, the 12 reagents listed in appendix A and their color reactions listed in table 1 are included for informational purposes only. A kit may contain any reagent or group of reagents that meet(s) the requirements of this standard.

3. DEFINITIONS

3.1 Munsell Color Charts

The Munsell Book of Color (Volumes 1 and 2) is a master atlas of color. Munsell color standards are made by applying a stable coating to a paper or polymer substrate using the most stable colorants available. The colors are made according to the specifications contained in the final report of the subcommittee of the Optical Society of America on the spacing of Munsell colors, J. Opt. Soc. Am., 33, 385–418 (1943). Samples of each production lot are measured by spectrophotometry and are visually inspected at the time of production. The collection displays nearly 1 600 color chips, arranged according to the Munsell color-order system. Each page presents one hue, and there are 40 pages, each 2.5 hue steps apart. On each page, the chips are arranged by Munsell value and chroma. The standard way to describe a color using Munsell notations is to write the numeric designation for the Munsell hue (H) and the numeric designation for value (V) and chroma (C) in the form of H V/C.

3.2 Centroid Color Charts

The Centroid Color Charts are a collection of charts, published by the Inter-Society Color Council (ISCC) and the National Institute of Standards and Technology (NIST), formally, the National Bureau of Standards (NBS), that logically group and illustrate colors. There is a chart for each color hue. On each chart, color saturation increases from left to right and color lightness increases from bottom to top. The charts are identified as NBS Standard Reference Material 2106. These charts are no longer available for purchase and have been replaced by the Munsell Color Charts. The numbers and color descriptions listed in table 1 of NILECJ-STD–0604.00 and NIJ Standard–0605.00 were taken from this chart. The NBS numbers are obsolete and are no longer considered to be the international standard for color. Therefore, these numbers are listed for historical purposes only.

3.3 Final Color

The final color was defined as the color (generally formed within 1 min or 2 min) that remained after any intermediate colors, produced by the addition of a reagent to a drug or other substance, have disappeared.

4. REQUIREMENTS

4.1 User Information

The kit shall include the following information.

4.1.1 Drugs Detected

A list of the drugs for which each reagent in the kit can be used to make a tentative identification.

4.1.2 Instructions

Clear instructions for performing the chemical test and for interpreting the results, including the time for the final color to appear.

Table 1. Final colors produced by reagents A.1 through A.12 with various drugs and other substances

	Analyte	Solvent	ISCC-NIST**	Color	Munsell
A.1	Benzphetamine HCl	CHCl₃	168	Brilliant greenish blue	5B 7/8
A.1	Brompheniramine Maleate	CHCl₃	168	Brilliant greenish blue	5B 6/10
A.1	Chlordiazepoxide HCl	CHCl₃	168	Brilliant greenish blue	2.5B 6/8
A.1	Chlorpromazine HCl	CHCl₃	168	Brilliant greenish blue	5B 6/10
A.1	Cocaine HCl	CHCl₃	169	Strong greenish blue	5B 5/10
A.1	Diacetylmorphine HCl	CHCl₃	169	Strong greenish blue	7.5B 6/10
A.1	Doxepin HCl	CHCl₃	168	Brilliant greenish blue	5B 6/10
A.1	Ephedrine HCl	CHCl₃	169	Strong greenish blue	5B 5/10
A.1	Hydrocodone tartrate	CHCl₃	168	Brilliant greenish blue	5B 6/8
A.1	Meperidine HCl	CHCl₃	169	Strong greenish blue	5B 5/10
A.1	Methadone HCl*	CHCl₃	168	Brilliant greenish blue	5B 6/10
A.1	Methylphenidate HCl	CHCl₃	168	Brilliant greenish blue	10BG 6/8
A.1	Phencyclidine HCl	CHCl₃	169	Strong greenish blue	5B 5/10
A.1	Procaine HCl*	CHCl₃	169	Strong greenish blue	5B 5/10
A.1	Propoxyphene HCl*	CHCl₃	169	Strong greenish blue	5B 5/10
A.1	Pseudoephedrine HCl	CHCl₃	169	Strong greenish blue	5B 5/10
A.1	Quinine HCl	CHCl₃	178	Strong blue	2.5PB 5/12
A.2	Amobarbital	CHCl₃	222	Light purple	5P 7/8
A.2	Pentobarbital*	CHCl₃	222	Light purple	5P 7/8
A.2	Phenobarbital*	CHCl₃	222	Light purple	5P 7/8
A.2	Secobarbital*	CHCl₃	222	Light purple	5P 7/8
A.3	Mace[5]	crystals	237[1]	Strong reddish purple	2.5RP 5/12
			237[2]	Strong reddish purple	2.5RP 5/12
			221[3]	Very light purple	5P 8/4
A.3	Nutmeg	extract	244[1]	Pale reddish purple	10P 6/4
			244[2]	Pale reddish purple	10P 6/4
			261[3]	Light gray purplish red	5RP 7/4
A.3	Tea	extract	119[4]	Light yellow green	5GY 8/6
A.3	THC*	EtOH	204[1]	Gray purplish blue	7.5PB 4/4
			199[2]	Light purplish blue	7.5PB 7/8
			219[3]	Deep purple	7.5P 4/12
A.4	Acetaminophen	CHCl₃	107	Moderate olive	10Y 5/8
A.4	Aspirin	powder	127	Grayish olive green	2.5GY 4/2
A.4	Benzphetamine HCl*	CHCl₃	116	Brilliant yellow green	2.5GY 8/10
A.4	Brompheniramine Maleate	CHCl₃	50	Strong orange	7.5YR 7/14
A.4	Chlorpromazine HCl	CHCl₃	108	Dark olive	10Y 3/4
A.4	Cocaine HCl*	CHCl₃	69	Deep orange yellow	10YR 7/14
A.4	Codeine*	CHCl₃	108	Dark olive	10Y 3/4
A.4	Contac	powder	84	Strong yellow	2.5Y 6/10
A.4	d-Amphetamine HCl*	CHCl₃	164	Moderate bluish green	5BG 5/6
A.4	d-Methamphetamine HCl*	CHCl₃	137	Dark yellowish green	10GY 4/6
A.4	Diacetylmorphine HCl*	CHCl₃	43	Moderate reddish brown	10R 3/6

3

Table 1. Final colors produced by reagents A.1 through A.12 with various drugs and other substances-Continued

	Analyte	Solvent	ISCC-NIST**	Color	Munsell
A.4	Dimethoxy-meth HCl	CHCl₃	96	Dark olive brown	5Y 2/2
A.4	Doxepin HCl	CHCl₃	44	Dark reddish brown	10R 2/4
A.4	Dristan	powder	110	Grayish olive	7.5Y 4/4
A.4	Exedrine	powder	108	Dark olive	7.5Y 3/4
A.4	Mace⁵	crystals	125	Moderate olive green	5GY 4/8
A.4	MDA HCl	CHCl₃	193	Bluish black	10B 2/2
A.4	Mescaline HCl*	CHCl₃	78	Dark yellowish brown	10YR 3/4
A.4	Methadone HCl	CHCl₃	187	Dark grayish blue	5B 3/2
A.4	Methaqualone	CHCl₃	66	Very orange yellow	10YR 8/14
A.4	Methylphenidate HCl	CHCl₃	67	Brilliant orange yellow	2.5Y 8/10
A.4	Morphine monohydrate*	CHCl₃	47	Dark grayish reddish Brown	10R 3/2
A.4	Opium*	CHCl₃	59	Dark brown	7.5YR 2/4
A.4	Oxycodone HCl	CHCl₃	103	Dark greenish yellow	10Y 6/6
A.4	Procaine HCl	CHCl₃	51	Deep orange	5YR 5/12
A.4	Propoxyphene HCl	CHCl₃	44	Dark reddish brown	10R 2/4
A.4	Quinine HCl	CHCl₃	100	Deep greenish yellow	10Y 9/6
A.4	Salt	crystals	50	Strong orange	5YR 7/12
A.5	Aspirin	powder	13	Deep red	5R 3/10
A.5	Benzphetamine HCl*	CHCl₃	41	Deep reddish brown	7.5R 2/6
A.5	Chlorpromazine HCl	CHCl₃	256	Deep purplish red	2.5RP 3/8
A.5	Codeine*	CHCl₃	225	Very dark purple	7.5P 2/4
A.5	d-Amphetamine HCl*	CHCl₃	35 to 44	Strong reddish orange Dark reddish brown	10R 6/12 to 7.5R 2/4
A.5	d-Methamphetamine HCl*	CHCl₃	36 to 44	Deep reddish orange Dark reddish brown	10R 4/12 to 7.5R 2/4
A.5	Diacetylmorphine HCl*	CHCl₃	256	Deep purplish red	7.5RP 3/10
A.5	Dimethoxy-meth HCl	CHCl₃	107	Moderate olive	7.5Y 5/8
A.5	Doxepin HCl	CHCl₃	21	Blackish red	7.5R 2/2
A.5	Dristan	powder	20	Dark grayish red	5R 3/2
A.5	Exedrine	powder	16	Dark red	5R 3/8
A.5	LSD	CHCl₃	114	Olive black	10Y 2/2
A.5	Mace⁵	crystals	87	Moderate yellow	7Y 7/8
A.5	MDA HCl*	CHCl₃	267	Black	Black
A.5	Meperidine HCl	CHCl₃	56	Deep brown	5YR 3/6
A.5	Mescaline HCl*	CHCl₃	50	Strong orange	5YR 6/12
A.5	Methadone HCl	CHCl₃	28	Light yellowish pink	2.5YR 8/4
A.5	Methylphenidate HCl	CHCl₃	71	Moderate orange yellow	10YR 8/8
A.5	Morphine monohydrate*	CHCl₃	239	Very deep reddish purple	10P 3/6
A.5	Opium*	Powder	47	Dark grayish reddish Brown	10R 3/2
A.5	Oxycodone HCl*	CHCl₃	214	Pale violet	2.5P 6/4
A.5	Propoxyphene HCl	CHCl₃	230	Blackish purple	2.5RP 2/2
A.5	Sugar	crystals	59	Dark brown	5YR 2/4

Table 1. Final colors produced by reagents A.l through A.12 with various drugs and other substances-Continued

	Analyte	Solvent	ISCC-NIST**	Color	Munsell
A.6	Acetaminophen	CHCl₃	67	Brilliant orange yellow	2.5Y 8/12
A.6	Codeine*	CHCl₃	101	Light greenish yellow	7.5Y 9/6
A.6	Diacetylmorphine HCl*	CHCl₃	89	Pale yellow	5Y 9/6
A.6	Dimethoxy-meth HCl	CHCl₃	82	Very yellow	2.5Y 8/14
A.6	Doxepin HCl	CHCl₃	83	Brilliant yellow	5Y 8.5/8
A.6	Dristan	powder	51	Deep orange	5YR 6/12
A.6	Exedrine	powder	67	Brilliant orange yellow	2.5Y 8/12
A.6	LSD	CHCl₃	55	Strong brown	5YR 5/10
A.6	Mace⁵	crystals	102	Moderate greenish yellow	10Y 7/6
A.6	MDA HCl	CHCl₃	101	Light greenish yellow	7.5Y 9/6
A.6	Mescaline HCl*	CHCl₃	16	Dark red	5R 3/6
A.6	Morphine monohydrate*	CHCl₃	67	Brilliant orange yellow	2.5Y 8/12
A.6	Opium*	Powder	72	Dark orange yellow	10YR 6/10
A.6	Oxycodone HCl	CHCl₃	83	Brilliant yellow	5Y 8.5/8
A.7	LSD*	CHCl₃	219	Deep purple	7.5P 3/10
A.8	Acetaminophen	MEOH	103	Dark greenish yellow	10Y 6/10
A.8	Baking Soda	powder	51	Deep orange	5YR 6/14
A.8	Chlorpromazine HCl	MEOH	48	Very orange	5YR 7/14
A.8	Dristan	powder	200	Moderate purplish blue	10PB 4/2
A.8	Exedrine	powder	200	Moderate purplish blue	10PB 4/2
A.8	Morphine monohydrate*	MEOH	146	Dark green	5G 3/6
A.9	Aspirin	powder	228	Grayish purple	7.5P 5/2
A.9	Chlorpromazine HCl	CHCl₃	14	Very deep red	5R 3/10
A.9	Codeine*	CHCl₃	147	Very dark green	7.5G 2/6
A.9	Contac	powder	95	Moderate olive brown	2.5Y 4/6
A.9	Diacetylmorphine HCl*	CHCl₃	256	Deep purplish red	5RP 3/10
A.9	Dimethoxy-meth HCl	CHCl₃	115	Very yellow green	5GY 6/10
A.9	Doxepin HCl	CHCl₃	41	Deep reddish brown	7.5R 2/8
A.9	Dristan	powder	163	Light bluish green	5BG 7/6
A.9	Exedrine	powder	177	Brilliant blue	10B 6/10
A.9	LSD	CHCl₃	120	Moderate yellow green	5GY 6/6
A.9	Mace⁵	crystals	70	Light olive yellow	10YR 8/8
A.9	MDA HCl*	CHCl₃	157	Greenish black	7.5G 2/2
A.9	Morphine monohydrate*	CHCl₃	256	Deep purplish red	5RP 3/10
A.9	Opium*	Powder	65	Brownish black	7.5R 2/2
A.9	Oxycodone HCl	CHCl₃	84	Strong yellow	2.5Y 7/10
A.9	Propoxyphene HCl	CHCl₃	20	Dark grayish red	2.5R 3/2
A.9	Sugar	crystals	83	Brilliant yellow	5Y 8.5/8
A.10	Chlorpromazine HCl	CHCl₃	21	Blackish red	5R 2/2
A.10	Codeine*	CHCl₃	166	Very dark bluish green	2.5BG 2/4
A.10	Contac	powder	95	Moderate olive brown	2.5Y 4/6

Table 1. Final colors produced by reagents A.1 through A.12 with various drugs and other substances-Continued

	Analyte	Solvent	ISCC-NIST**	Color	Munsell
A.10	Diacetylmorphine HCl*	CHCl₃	161	Deep bluish green	2.5BG 3/8
A.10	Dimethoxy-meth HCl	CHCl₃	59	Dark brown	5YR 2/4
A.10	Doxepin HCl	CHCl₃	17	Very dark red	5R 2/4
A.10	Dristan	powder	94	Light olive brown	2.5Y 6/10
A.10	Exedrine	powder	91	Dark grayish yellow	5Y 6/4
A.10	Hydrocodone tartrate	CHCl₃	165	Dark bluish green	5BG 3/6
A.10	LSD	CHCl₃	157	Greenish black	7.5G 2/2
A.10	Mace⁵	crystals	111	Dark grayish olive	10Y 3/4
A.10	MDA HCl*	CHCl₃	166	Very dark bluish green	2.5BG 2/4
A.10	Mescaline HCl*	CHCl₃	107	Moderate olive	7.5Y 5/8
A.10	Morphine monohydrate*	CHCl₃	166	Very dark bluish green	2.5BG 2/4
A.10	Nutmeg	leaves	65	Brownish black	10YR 2/2
A.10	Opium*	Powder	114	Olive black	10Y 2/2
A.10	Oxycodone HCl	CHCl₃	107	Moderate olive	7.5Y 5/8
A.10	Propoxyphene HCl	CHCl₃	41	Deep reddish brown	10R 2/6
A.10	Sugar	crystals	98	Brilliant greenish yellow	10Y 8.5/10
A.11	Baking Soda	powder	181	Light blue	2.5PB 7/6
A.11	Exedrine	powder	144	Light green	5G 7/6
A.11	Pentobarbital*	CHCl₃	222	Light purple	7.5P 7/6
A.11	Phenobarbital*	CHCl₃	222	Light purple	7.5P 7/6
A.11	Secobarbital*	CHCl₃	222	Light purple	7.5P 7/6
A.11	Tea	leaves	120	Moderate yellow green	2.5GY 7/8
A.11	Tobacco	leaves	136	Moderate yellowish green	10GY 6/6
A.12	d-Methamphetamine HCl*	CHCl₃	183	Dark blue	2.5PB 2/6
A.12	Dimethoxy-meth HCl*	CHCl₃	179	Deep blue	2.5PB 3/8
A.12	MDMA HCl	CHCl₃	183	Dark blue	2.5PB 2/6
A.12	Methylphenidate HCl	CHCl₃	214	Pale violet	2.5P 6/4

* Usual kit reagent for that particular drug.

** Inter-Society Color Council and the National Institute of Standards and Technology (ISCC-NIST), formerly ISCC/NBS, National Bureau of Standards (NBS).

[1]Aqueous phase.

[2]Aqueous phase after chloroform extraction.

[3]Chloroform phase (marijuana extraction usually rapid compared to other materials).

[4]Not extracted into chloroform.

[5]2-Chloroacetophenone.

4.1.3 Safety Precautions

a) Warning of the hazards of the flammable and corrosive chemicals contained in the kit.
b) Steps to follow and antidotes to use if hazardous reagents are taken internally or come in contact with parts of the body or clothes.
c) Procedures for safely discarding used reagents and containers.

4.1.4 General

a) A statement that the kit is intended to be used for presumptive identification purposes only, and that all substances tested should be subjected to more definitive examination by qualified scientists in a properly equipped crime laboratory.
b) A statement that users of the kit should receive appropriate training in its use and should be taught that the reagents can give false-positive as well as false-negative results.
c) A discussion of the possibility of reagent and/or sample contamination and consequent misleading results.
d) A discussion of proper kit storage in buildings and vehicles.

4.2 Labeling

Each reagent container shall have a label that either directly or by reference:

a) Identifies the reagent.
b) Identifies the drug or drugs it can detect.
c) Is prominently marked "Danger" where appropriate.
d) Gives a discard date where appropriate.

4.3 Workmanship

Visual inspection of the kit shall show no broken or inoperative catches, hinges, or containers. There shall be no evidence of reagent leakage.

4.4 Safe-Disposal Materials

The kit shall contain chemicals for neutralizing strongly acidic and basic reagents and/or acid/base-resistant containers into which used reagents and containers can be deposited and safely disposed of at a later time in accordance with section 4.1.3.c.

4.5 Color Samples

The kit shall include samples or reproductions of the color or colors produced by each reagent in the kit when reacted with each drug listed on the reagent container label.

4.6 Test Color and Sensitivity

Each reagent in the kit shall produce the color or colors specified by the manufacturer in the form of color samples (sec. 4.5) or have the same color hue and color saturation as those colors, for each of five replicate tests, performed in accordance with section 5.2 at the drug detection limit listed in table 2 or specified by the manufacturer in accordance with section 4.7. If a reagent produces the same color with more than one drug, this test should be performed from only one of those reagent/drug combinations.

4.7 Drug Detection Limit

The manufacturer shall specify the drug detection limit, determined in accordance with section 5.3, for each drug/reagent combination listed on a reagent container label, other than those listed in table 2.

4.8 Specificity

The kit shall include sufficient reagents to permit differentiation between each drug listed in accordance with section 4.1.1 and the other substances listed in table 3. The differentiation may be accomplished by the use of a single reagent or by a combination of reagents. Acceptable differentiation occurs if the final colors of the test are not in the color vicinity of one another when checked in accordance with section 5.4.

5. TEST METHODS

5.1 General Test Conditions

At the time of the tests, the ambient temperature shall be between 10°C and 40 °C (50 °F and 104 °F); the relative humidity shall be between 10 percent and 90 percent. Recommended Safety Precautions (see app. B) and Storage Precautions (see app. C) shall be followed.

5.2 Test Color

Place 500 μg of the drug, either as powder or dissolved in chloroform, in each of three wells of the porcelain test plate (except for app. A.3, where glass culture tubes are used). If the kit is packaged with the reagents in sealed glass tubes for single test field purposes, break the reagent tubes in suitable individual containers such as small beakers or test tubes. Use a disposable pasteur-type pipette to transfer one drop (approximately 0.1 mL) of each reagent being tested, in the sequence specified by the manufacturer if appropriate, to each of the three wells[1]. Compare the color or colors produced within the specified time limits to those provided by the

---

[1] When two or more reagents are used sequentially, transfer the minimum number of drops of each reagent equivalent to the ratio specified by the manufacturer (i.e., three drops to one drop, etc.).

manufacturer in accordance with section 4.5, and determine whether the colors are essentially the same.

If the colors do not match, check the drug solution and test procedure by repeating the above procedure using fresh reagent prepared as directed in appendix A or by the manufacturer. This paragraph is not applicable to reagents not listed in appendix A unless information similar to that in appendix A is supplied by the manufacturer.

5.3 Drug Detection Limit Determination

Prepare a 1.0 µg/µL solution (or lower if necessary) of the selected drug in chloroform or methanol. Using a micropipette, transfer five samples of this solution to the test wells or tubes. Add reagent as described in section 5.2. Change the quantity of drug transferred by varying either the solution concentration or the volume transferred, and repeat the test until the smallest mass of transferred drug is determined, to one significant figure, for which five out of five color changes are observed. As a safety factor, multiply this quantity by 10, and use the product as the operational drug detection limit.

5.4 Specificity Test

For each reagent in the kit other than those listed in appendix A, determine the final color, if any, when mixed with each substance listed in table 3.

Table 2. Drug detection limits

Reagent	Analyte	Drug Detection Limit (µg)
A.1	Cocaine HCl	60
A.1	Methadone HCl	250
A.2	Amobarbital	25
A.2	Pentobarbital	10
A.2	Phenobarbital	15
A.2	Secobarbital	25
A.3	THC	5
A.4	d-Amphetamine HCl	20
A.4	d-Methamphetamine HCl	100
A.4	Codeine	20
A.4	Diacetylmorphine HCl	20
A.4	Morphine monohydrate	5
A.5	d-Amphetamine HCl	10
A.5	Codeine	1
A.5	Diacetylmorphine HCl	10
A.5	LSD	5
A.5	Mescaline HCl	10
A.5	Methadone HCl	20
A.5	d-Methamphet HCl	5
A.5	Morphine monohydrate	5
A.6	Mescaline HCl	1
A.7	LSD	6
A.8	Morphine monohydrate	200
A.9	Codeine	50
A.9	Diacetylmorphine HCl	200
A.9	LSD	50
A.9	Mescaline HCl	100
A.9	Morphine monohydrate	25
A.10	Codeine	25
A.10	Diacetylmorphine HCl	200
A.10	LSD	50
A.10	Mescaline HCl	50
A.10	Morphine monohydrate	50
A.11	Phenobarb	1000
A.12	d-Methamphetamine HCl	10
A.12	Methylphenidate HCl	300

*The solvent is $CHCl_3$ except for A.8, which is methanol.

Table 3. Specificity of color tests

(+) Indicates that a color reaction occurs[1]

	REAGENT											
	A.1	A.2	A.3	A.4	A.5	A.6	A.7	A.8	A.9	A.10	A.11	A.12
Acetominophen	-	-	-	+	-	+	-	+	-	-	-	-
Alprazolam	-	-	-	-	-	-	-	-	-	-	-	-
Aspirin	-	-	-	+	+	-	-	-	+	-	-	-
Baking Soda	-	-	-	-	-	-	-	+	-	-	+	-
Brompheniramine Maleate	+	-	-	+	-	-	-	-	-	-	-	-
Chlordiazepoxide HCl	+	-	-	-	-	-	-	-	-	-	-	-
Chlorpromazine HCl	+	-	-	+	+	+	-	+	+	+	-	-
Contac	-	-	-	+	-	-	-	-	+	+	-	-
Diazepam	-	-	-	-	-	-	-	-	-	-	-	-
Doxepin HCl	+	-	-	+	+	+	-	-	+	+	-	-
Dristan	-	-	-	+	+	+	-	+	+	+	-	-
Ephedrine HCl	+	-	-	-	-	-	-	-	-	-	-	-
Exedrine	-	-	-	+	+	+	-	+	+	+	+	-
Hydrocodone tartrate	+	-	-	-	-	-	-	-	+	-	-	-
Mace[2]	-	-	+	+	+	+	-	-	+	+	-	-
Meperidine HCl	+	-	-	-	+	-	-	-	-	-	-	-
Methaqualone	-	-	-	+	-	-	-	-	-	-	-	-
Methylphenidate HCl	+	-	-	+	+	-	-	-	-	-	-	+
Nutmeg[2]	-	-	+	-	-	-	-	-	-	+	-	-
Phencyclidine HCl	+	-	-	-	-	-	-	-	-	-	-	-
Propoxyphene HCl	+	-	-	+	+	-	-	-	+	+	-	-
Pseudoephedrine HCl	+	-	-	-	-	-	-	-	-	-	-	-
Quinine HCl	+	-	-	+	-	-	-	-	-	-	-	-
Salt	-	-	-	+	-	-	-	-	-	-	-	-
Sugar	-	-	-	-	+	-	-	-	+	+	-	-
Tea[2]	-	-	+	-	-	-	-	-	-	-	+	-
Tobacco	-	-	-	-	-	-	-	-	-	-	+	-

[1]Substances that gave no colors with these reagents are: D-galactose, glucose, mannitol, oregano, rosemary, and thyme.

[2]Tea, mace, and nutmeg may interfere with the Duquenios test but not the Duquenois-Levine modified test (A.3).

11

APPENDIX A–REAGENTS

A.1 Cobalt Thiocyanate

Dissolve 2.0 g of cobalt (II) thiocyanate in 100 mL of distilled water.

A.2 Dille-Koppanyi Reagent, Modified

Solution A: Dissolve 0.1 g of cobalt (II) acetate dihydrate in 100 mL of methanol. Add 0.2 mL of glacial acetic acid and mix.
Solution B: Add 5 mL of isopropylamine to 95 mL of methanol.

Procedure: Add 2 volumes of solution A to the drug, followed by 1 volume of solution B.

A.3 Duquenois-Levine Reagent, Modified

Solution A: Add 2.5 mL of acetaldehyde and 2.0 g of vanillin to 100 mL of 95 percent ethanol.
Solution B: Concentrated hydrochloric acid.
Solution C: Chloroform.

Procedure: Add 1 volume of solution A to the drug and shake for 1 min. Then add 1 volume of solution B. Agitate gently, and determine the color produced. Add 3 volumes of solution C and note whether the color is extracted from the mixture to A and B.

A.4 Mandelin Reagent

Dissolve 1.0 g of ammonium vanadate in 100 mL of concentrated sulfuric acid.

A.5 Marquis Reagent

Carefully add 100 mL of concentrated sulfuric acid to 5 mL of 40 percent formaldehyde (v:v, formaldehyde:water).

A.6 Nitric Acid

Concentrated nitric acid.

A.7 *Para*-Dimethylaminobenzaldehyde (*p*-DMAB)

Add 2.0 g of *p*-DMAB to 50 mL of 95 percent ethanol and 50 mL of concentrated hydrochloric acid.

A.8 Ferric Chloride

Dissolve 2.0 g of anhydrous ferric chloride or 3.3 g of ferric chloride hexahydrate in 100 mL of distilled water.

A.9 Froede Reagent

Dissolve 0.5 g of molybdic acid or sodium molybate in 100 mL of hot concentrated sulfuric acid.

A.10 Mecke Reagent

Dissolve 1.0 g of selenious acid in 100 mL of concentrated sulfuric acid.

A.11 Zwikker Reagent

Solution A: Dissolve 0.5 g of copper (II) sulfate pentahydrate in 100 mL of distilled water.
Solution B: Add 5 mL of pyridine to 95 mL of chloroform.

Procedure: Add 1 volume of solution A to the drug, followed by 1 volume of solution B.

A.12 Simon's Reagent

Solution A: Dissolve 1 g of sodium nitroprusside in 50 mL of distilled water and add 2 mL of acetaldehyde to the solution with thorough mixing.
Solution B: 2 percent sodium carbonate in distilled water.

Procedure: Add 1 volume of solution A to the drug, followed by 2 volumes of solution B.

APPENDIX B–SAFETY PRECAUTIONS

A.1 Cobalt Thiocyanate

1. Cobalt Thiocyanate – HARMFUL. Harmful if swallowed. Readily absorbed through the skin. Target organs: lungs, thyroid. Wear suitable protective clothing and gloves.

A.2 Dille-Koppanyi Reagent, Modified

1. Cobalt (II) acetate dihydrate – TOXIC. May cause cancer. May cause heritable genetic damage. Harmful by inhalation, contact with skin, and if swallowed. May cause sensitization by skin contact. Causes irritation. Target organs: lungs, thyroid. In case of accident or if you feel unwell, seek medical advice immediately. In case of contact with eyes, rinse immediately with plenty of water and seek medical advice. Wear suitable protective clothing, gloves, and eye/face protection. Do not breathe dust.

2. Methanol - POISON, FLAMMABLE.[2] Flammable liquid and vapor. Cumulative poison. Harmful if inhaled. May be fatal or cause blindness if swallowed. Can cause eye, skin, or respiratory system irritation. Wear suitable protective clothing and gloves.

3. Glacial acetic acid – ACID.[3] Combustible, flammable, corrosive, organic acid. Causes severe burns. Harmful in contact with skin. Lachrymator. Target organs: teeth, kidneys. Keep away from sources of ignition. In case of accident or if you feel unwell, seek medical advice immediately. In case of contact with eyes, rinse immediately with plenty of water and seek medical advice. Wear suitable protective clothing, gloves, and eye/face protection. Incompatible with carbonates, hydroxides, many oxides and phosphates, etc.

4. Isopropylamine – FLAMMABLE.[2] Corrosive. Causes burns. Toxic by inhalation, in contact with skin, and if swallowed. Keep away from sources of ignition. Take precautionary measures against static discharges. In case of accident or if you feel unwell, seek medical advice immediately. In case of contact with eyes, rinse immediately with plenty of water and seek medical advice. Wear suitable protective clothing, gloves, and eye/face protection.

A.3 Duquenois-Levine Reagent, Modified

1. Acetaldehyde - EXTREMELY FLAMMABLE,[2] TOXIC. May cause cancer. May cause heritable genetic damage. Harmful by inhalation, in contact with skin, and if swallowed. May cause sensitization by inhalation and skin contact. Possible risk of harm to unborn child. Causes severe irritation. Lachrymator. Photosensitizer. Target organs: kidneys, liver. May develop pressure. Keep away from sources of ignition. In case of contact with eyes, rinse immediately

with plenty of water and seek medical advice. Wear suitable protective clothing, gloves, and eye/face protection.

2. Vanilin – none.

3. Ethanol – FLAMMABLE.[2] May irritate in body tissues. Use with adequate ventilation. Avoid breathing vapor. Do not get on eyes, skin, or clothing. Wash thoroughly after handling. Do not swallow or inhale. Wear suitable protective clothing and gloves.

4. Hydrochloric acid – ACID,[3] TOXIC, CORROSIVE. Liquid and mist cause severe burns to all body tissue. May be fatal if swallowed or inhaled. Inhalation may cause lung damage. Do not get on skin or clothing. Wash thoroughly after handling. Wear suitable protective clothing, gloves, and eye/face protection. Use only with adequate ventilation.

5. Chloroform – FLAMMABLE,[2] TOXIC, POISON. Suspected cancer hazard. Exposure can cause damage to liver, kidneys, and central nervous system (CNS). Harmful if swallowed. Causes eye irritation. Harmful to skin and respiratory system. Toxic and corrosive gases are formed on contact with flames or hot glowing surfaces. Wear suitable protective clothing and gloves.

A.4 Mandelin Reagent

1. Ammonium vanadate - TOXIC. Toxic by inhalation, in contact with skin, and if swallowed. Irritating to eyes and respiratory system. Risk of serious damage to eyes. Possible risk of irreversible effects. Possible mutagen. In case of accident or if you feel unwell, seek medical advice immediately. In case of contact with eyes, rinse immediately with plenty of water and seek medical advice. Wear suitable protective clothing, gloves, and eye/face protection.

2. Sulfuric acid – OXIDIZER,[1] ACID,[3] TOXIC, CORROSIVE. Liquid and mist cause severe burns to all body tissue. May be fatal if swallowed. Harmful if inhaled. Inhalation may case lung damage. Do not get liquid in eyes, on skin, or clothing. Wash thoroughly after handling. Avoid breathing vapors. Use with adequate ventilation. Do not add water to contents while in container because of violent reaction. Store in tightly closed container. Wear suitable protective clothing and gloves.

A.5 Marquis Reagent

1. Sulfuric Acid - see A.4.

2. Formaldehyde - TOXIC. May cause cancer. May cause heritable genetic damage. Toxic by inhalation, in contact with skin, and if swallowed. Causes burns. May cause sensitization by inhalation and skin contact. Readily absorbed through skin. Lachrymator.

Combustible. Target organs: eyes, kidneys. Wear suitable protective clothing and gloves.

A.6 Nitric Acid

1. Nitric acid – OXIDIZER,[1] ACID.[3] Do not breathe vapor. Do not get in eyes or on skin or clothing. Keep in tightly closed, light-resistant container. In case of contact, immediately flush eyes or skin with plenty of water for at least 15 min. Causes severe burns. Vapor extremely hazardous. May cause nitrous gas poisoning. Spillage may cause fire or liberate dangerous gas. May be fatal if swallowed.

A.7 *Para*-Dimethylaminobenzaldehyde (*p*-DMAB)

1. *p*-DMAB - HARMFUL. Harmful if swallowed, irritating to eyes, respiratory system, and skin. In case of contact with eyes, rinse immediately with plenty of water and seek medical advice. Wear suitable protective clothing, gloves, and eye/face protection.

2. Ethanol - See A-3.

3. Hydrochloric acid - See A.3.

A.8 Ferric Chloride

1. Ferric chloride – OXIDIZER,[1] CORROSIVE. Causes burns. Harmful by inhalation, contact with skin, and if swallowed. In case of contact with eyes, rinse immediately with plenty of water and seek medical advice. Take off all contaminated clothing immediately. Wear suitable protective clothing, gloves, and eye/face protection.

A.9 Froede Reagent

1. Sodium molybdate - IRRITANT. Irritating to eyes, respiratory system, and skin. In case of contact with eyes, rinse immediately with plenty of water and seek medical advice. Wear suitable protective clothing, gloves, and eye/face protection.

2. Sulfuric acid - See A.5.

A.10 Mecke Reagent

1. Selenious acid – OXIDIZER,[1] TOXIC. Highly toxic. Contact with combustible material may cause fire. Toxic by inhalation, in contact with skin, and if swallowed. Irritating to eyes, respiratory system, and skin. Target organs: liver, heart. Keep away from combustible material. In case of contact with eyes, rinse immediately with plenty of water and seek medical advice. Take off immediately all contaminated clothing. Wear suitable protective clothing, gloves, and eye/face protection.

2. Sulfuric acid - See A.5.

A.11 Zwikker Reagent

1. Copper (II) sulfate pentahydrate - HARMFUL, TOXIC. May impair fertility. Possible risk of harm to unborn child. Harmful if swallowed. Risk of serious damage to eyes. Irritating to respiratory system, and skin. May cause sensitization by skin contact. Target organs: liver, kidneys. In case of accident or if you feel unwell, seek medical advice immediately. In case of contact with eyes, rinse immediately with plenty of water and seek medical advice. Wear suitable protective clothing, gloves, and eye/face protection. Do not breathe dust.

2. Pyridine – FLAMMABLE.[2] Keep away from heat, sparks, and flames. Use only with adequate ventilation. Vapors may be explosive. Wear suitable protective clothing. Harmful if inhaled. Liquid causes eye irritation. May be harmful if swallowed or absorbed through the skin. Avoid breathing vapors. Avoid contact with eyes, and skin. Wash thoroughly after handling.

3. Chloroform - See A.3.

A.12 Simon's Reagent

1. Sodium nitroprusside - VERY TOXIC. Very toxic by inhalation, contact with skin, and if swallowed. Target organs: blood. In case of accident or if you feel unwell, seek medical advice immediately. In case of contact with eyes, rinse immediately with plenty of water and seek medical advice. Wear suitable protective clothing, gloves, and eye/face protection. Do not breathe dust.

2. Pyridine - See A.11.

3. Acetaldehyde - See A.3.

4. Sodium carbonate – BASE.[4] Harmful if swallowed. May cause skin irritation. Harmful if inhaled. Wash thoroughly after handling.

APPENDIX C–STORAGE PRECAUTIONS

[1]OXIDIZERS:

    Store in a cool, dry place.

    Keep away from flammable and combustible materials (paper, wood, etc.)

    Keep away from reducing agents such as zinc, alkaline metals, and formic acid.

[2]FLAMMABLES:

    Store in approved safety cans or cabinets.

    Segregate from oxidizing acids and oxidizers.

    Keep away any source of ignition: flames, localized heat, or sparks.

    Safety cans or drums containing flammable liquids should be grounded and bonded when being used.

    Keep firefighting equipment readily available.

    Have spill cleanup materials handy.

    Store highly volatile flammable liquids in a specially equipped refrigerator.

[3]ACIDS:

    Store large bottles of acids on low shelf or in acid cabinets.

    Segregate oxidizing acids from organic acids, flammable and combustible materials.

    Segregate acids from bases and active metals such as sodium, potassium, magnesium, etc.

    Segregate acids from chemicals that could generate toxic gases upon contact such as sodium cyanide, iron sulfide, etc.

    Use bottle carriers for transporting acid bottles.

    Have spill control pillows or acid neutralizers available in case of acid spills.

[4]BASES:

    Segregate bases from acids.

    Store solutions of inorganic hydroxides in polyethylene containers.

    Have spill control pillows or caustic neutralizers available for caustic spills.

U.S. Department of Justice
Office of Justice Programs
810 Seventh Street N.W.
Washington, DC 20531

Janet Reno
Attorney General

Daniel Marcus
Acting Associate Attorney General

Mary Lou Leary
Acting Assistant Attorney General

Julie E. Samuels
Acting Director, National Institute of Justice

Office of Justice Programs	**National Institute of Justice**
World Wide Web Site:	**World Wide Web Site:**
http://www.ojp.usdoj.gov	*http://www.ojp.usdoj.gov/nij*

www.ingramcontent.com/pod-product-compliance
Lightning Source LLC
Chambersburg PA
CBHW080627180526

45168CB00007B/3080